Touching the Heart of God

Special Edition, Volume 1

Cindy Barrineau Curtis

Published by Cindy Barrineau Curtis, 2025.

First published in The United States of America 2007

By Cindy B Curtis

ISBN:979-8-9884509-2-4[1]

Cover Art: pexels

1. https://www.myidentifiers.com/title_registration?isbn=979-8-9884509-2-4&icon_type=Assigned

TOUCHING THE HEART OF GOD

First edition. February 7, 2025.

ISBN: 979-8988450924

Written by Cindy Barrineau Curtis.

Also by Cindy Barrineau Curtis

Special Edition
Touching the Heart of God

Standalone
When the Breeze Whispers: Find Your Truth

Watch for more at https://cindybcurtis.com.

Table of Contents

For all those who are searching...

Trust in the Lord with all your heart and lean not on your own understanding. In all your ways acknowledge him, and he will direct your path.

Proverbs 3:5-6

Acceptance

Where do I belong?
where do I fit?
am I just a part of a puzzle?
Undiscovered
a place for me must lie around the next bend
must be at the next junction
Mold me
Heal me
Abide in me
Love me
A child
who is wandering.

Read Psalm 40: 8

"I desire to do your will, O my God; your law is within my heart."

Prayer:

God, I do not know what You have in Your will for me. I see where I am headed for just this moment, just this day. That is enough. Your plan for me is perfect. I can't question why. Please, Father, give me the grace to accept what You have for me. Give me the patience to wait on You. Thank You for loving me enough to guide me in all my ways. Amen.

Adoration

The glory of the Lord surrounds me
in the still quiet morning,
in the crash of the thunderstorm,
in the delicate lilt of the bird's song
in the majestic color of the flowers
in the rain sparkled evening.
I hear Your voice
as a whisper from a loving Father
"I love you, my child."
and I answer
in humble adoration
"Thank you, God."

Read Psalm 19

"The heavens proclaim the glory of God; the skies proclaim the work of his hands."

Prayer:

Heavenly Father, when I look upon the glory of Your works, I am so awed by the wonder of all You have created. The vivid colors of the flowers in bloom, the mighty ocean waves, the quiet of a gently falling rain, the highest majestic peak, all surpass my ability to fathom their wonders. You are the Almighty God, the Father and Creator. I worship and adore You, Lord, with highest praise.

I rest assured with the knowledge that You love me in the midst of all the beauty and wonder of Your creation. You formed me and love me as Your precious child. Thank You, Father. Amen.

Anger

The hot noise fills the space
inside my head -
a raging bull
ready to charge
WHY?
explodes from my lips
in anguish and pain
an unanswered question
one word
so full of darkness
and empty promises
will I ever be able to let go?
...and heal.

Read James 1:19-21

"My dear brothers, take note of this: Everyone should be quick to listen, slow to speak and slow to become angry."

Prayer:

Lord of all, You know my heart is consumed with anger. I don't understand the depth of my emotions. I feel so out of control. I pray for peace, and for your power to overtake the feelings I have experienced. Restore me to calm. When I rage and shout "Why?" Lord, I know You hear me. I understand that the answers to all of my questions may not be for me to know right now. Help me in my anger to accept that, Lord, and to rely on You. Thank You for loving me, even when I am so upset. Thank You for taking my anger and working in me to restore peace. Amen.

Blessing

The joy
that wells up inside me
originates
in the endless waters of your love.
Wash over me
with the waves of blessing
more valuable
than any possession
lasting and true
grace
peace
and love
poured out for all times.

Read Matthew 5

"Rejoice and be glad for great is your reward in heaven..."

Prayer:

Dear Lord, You teach us that blessings pour out on us when we live as Your children. I praise Your name and thank You for all the blessings You have given me. From the ability to wake this day and praise You, to the joy Your love brings to my heart, I thank You. I continue to need your blessings, Lord. I trust that You know what is best for me better than I do. I wait on Your blessings with a grateful, overflowing heart. Amen.

Change

It is too hard,
too much to ask,
too overwhelming for me.
The tasks set before me
loom large and monstrous,
too enormous for me to conquer.
I don't have the energy to try.
Change me.
Change my attitude.
Change my resistance.
...so that I am able to
conquer change.

Read Ecclesiastes 3:1-8

"There is a time for everything and a season for every activity under heaven."

Prayer:

Oh, Lord, change is so hard. I don't want to go through this trial. It's too difficult to make the changes I need to make. Please, Lord, help me. Guide me to break down the tasks before me into small parts, so You and I may handle them one at a time. I become so overwhelmed, and I give up before I even start. Help me today to move on with one small step, then another and another. Most of all, help me to accept and embrace change with Your love and strength to hold me up. Amen.

Comfort

The pain is
a tangible force that I cannot tame.
The depth of my feelings
Are unmanageable filling me with dread.
I wait for it to pass,
It walks on my heart
tramples my soul
torments me night and day.
I long for respite, for a moment of normalcy.
I wait
wounded and fearful
for the promised hope.

Read Matthew 11: 28-30

"Come to me all you who are weary and burdened, and I will give you rest."

Prayer:

Holy Spirit, You are the Great Comforter. You take my hurt. Surround me with Your love. Take me now. Wrap Your arms of love around me. I need the pain to ease. I need Your love to heal me. Mend the brokenness of my spirit. You are the balm for my wounds, and the comfort in my despair. I feel so helpless. Your presence offers me hope. For the next few minutes, let Your peace flow over me in a mighty way. You relieve my worries. Take my burden. Lift my load as only You can. Amen.

Confession

The shame I feel
must be apparent to all
who see my face
I cannot hide
the feelings of inadequacy
I cannot believe
that I have sinned again
I am so weak, so easily tempted
The remorse flows from me
as I fall on my knees

hiding my face on the floor

In agony I whisper,
"I'm sorry, please, forgive me."

Read Numbers 5: 5-7

" ...'When a man or woman wrongs another in any way and is unfaithful to the Lord, that person is guilty and must confess the sin he has committed."

Prayer:

Loving God, I confess that I have sinned. In my weakness, I disappointed You. I know how to act, Father, but I let myself slip. Forgive me, Lord. Take this sin away from me. I am so sorry for my weakness and for my sin. I know that with Your strength to support me, I can overcome any temptation I may encounter. I ask You to help me. I kneel before You with a humble, contrite heart as Your love covers my sin. Amen.

Conflict

Turmoil
Anguish
Pain
Bitterness
Confrontations building
and releasing
hiding
and storming in.
What waits
under the emotional upheaval
I cannot see.
Please,
open my eyes.

Read 2 Timothy 2:24-26

"And the Lord's servant must not quarrel; instead he must be kind to everyone, able to teach, not resentful."

Prayer:

Lord, I'm not sure the words to use to resolve the conflict that I'm feeling. The pain and anger are real and ever present. Your word instructs me not to quarrel. Show me Your way through this problem. Help me resolve it as You would with grace and peace. If I can't, then help me wait until I can. Keep me from adding more bitterness in my weakness. Thank you, Lord. Amen.

Confusion

Where do I turn?
Whom do I trust ?
How do I
discern the way, or
understand the truth?
Worry depletes
leaving me dry
as weak as old bones in the bitter sun.
Help me now.
Calm my fears.
Lead me.
to Your perfect peace.

Read James 1:5-7

"If any of you lacks wisdom, he should ask God who gives generously to all without finding fault, and it will be given to him."

Prayer:

God of all, show me Your way. I'm confused and unsure. I come to You asking, seeking wisdom, and answers. Please guide me. Help me discern Your will. I know You hear my plea. I know You will answer me. If I don't hear a definite yes or no, Lord, I will wait. For I know waiting on You is the best way for me to gain the wisdom that I need. Gratefully, I lift praise to You for all that You give to me. Amen.

Direction

The road
before me
is an unknown
that I must travel down
Unaware.
Unafraid.
yet I hesitate
Which way do I choose?
Indecision cripples me
so I stop
ask again for guidance
for clear direction.

Read Proverbs 3:5-6

"Trust in the Lord with all your heart and lean not on your own understanding; in all your ways acknowledge him and he will make your paths straight."

Prayer:

Lord, you have searched me. You know me better than I know myself. I do not know which way I am to go. I find myself at a cross roads. I have to make a decision. Lord, I come to You seeking Your will. You know what is best and perfect for me. I do trust You with all my heart. Be with me, God, as I choose the direction You have chosen for me to follow. I praise You and acknowledge You in all my ways. Amen.

Discernment

Decisions
weigh heavily
on my heart.
the enormity of it all
can overwhelm me
can leave me feeling helpless.
Take me as your child.
Oh God
lead me
to Your way.

Read Philippians 1: 9-11

"So that you may be able to discern what is best, and be blameless until the day of Christ."

Prayer:

Holy Spirit, dwell in me. Take away my confusion. Show me the way You would have me to go, the life You would have me to lead. I find the enormity of the tasks before me overwhelming. I ask You to break them down into small manageable parts for me to handle surrounded by Your loving grace; one decision at a time. Thank You, Loving Spirit, for Your help and counsel. Amen.

Discipline

Help me
when I need more
than I am able to manage
when I go wrong
Correct me
Paths ahead loom
as unclear murky water
and lead me to errors
I do not want to do wrong intentionally
yet, in my haste,
I can act rashly
Slow me down.
Correct my impulsiveness.

Read Hebrews 12:5-12

"Endure hardship as a discipline; God is treating you as sons and daughters."

Prayer:

God, You are The Father of Creation, The Wise Counselor, and The Great I Am. You know what is best for me even when I think I am in control. I know I am not, but You are. Lord, guide me in Your path. Teach me Your ways that I may walk in Your direction. Let me know this present path may seem unclear. Let me see the purpose You have set out for me. Your discipline is for my good. As a father directs his children, direct me. Amen.

Doubt

Uncertainty cripples me
Did I understand correctly?
Am I sure?
Do I waiver back and forth?
Does the needle of doubt
prick at my heart
cause me to suspect,
to question,
to second guess,
What is truth?

Read James 1:6

"But when he asks, he must believe and not doubt, because he who doubts is like a wave of the sea, blown and tossed by the wind."

Prayer:

Lord God, help me to be strong in my faith. I know Your way is the perfect way, yet I am doubtful. I have tried to release my concerns to You relying on my faith and not waiver. I'm finding it so difficult to trust and to believe that You hear me. I seek You, Lord, with all that I am. I ask You to take this doubt from me. Show me what You have in store for me. I trust You. I give my doubt to You with gratitude that You will take care of me. Love me through my pain and confusion. Amen.

Encouragement

An outstretched hand
to clasp my hesitant one,
a hug given spontaneously,
a pat on the back
when I least expect it.
A slow smile from across a room,
A warm summer rain
filling my heart
with God's peaceful joy.

Read Romans 15:5

"May the God who gives endurance and encouragement give you a spirit of unity among yourselves as you follow Christ Jesus."

Prayer:

Dear Jesus, Your love and strength encourages me when I'm weary and weak. Thank you, Lord. Help me to rely on that love and strength in any situation. Help me to know without any doubts. You are my encourager. You want me to do well. Even more, Lord, help me to encourage others in the strength of Your love. Let me be the source of hope for those who are feeling hopeless. Fill my soul with Your encouragement. Provide a chance for me to encourage someone today in Your name. Amen.

Faith

Assurance
The knowledge that I am watched over
by a loving God
The joy of heartfelt peace
The promise of tears wiped away
Hurts wrapped in love
Strength to move forward
one tiny step at a time
Faith as small as that
can do mighty things.

Read Matthew 17:18-21

"I tell you the truth, if you have faith as small as a mustard seed, you can say to this mountain, 'Move from here to there' and it will move. Nothing will be impossible for you."

Prayer:

Dear Jesus, teach me to have the faith of which You speak. I can be so weak in my faith walk. Show me how to believe. Help me to know that You are God of all, including the weak. By faith, You will strengthen me. Equip me for the work You have laid out for me to accomplish. Increase Your kingdom. I want to be strong, but I need Your help. Come to me now, Lord. Fill me with the power of Your Spirit. Grow my faith so I can pass your love on to others. Amen.

Fear

Darkness and despair
walk behind me
threatening to overwhelm me
and render me helpless
I am so afraid
so tired
so weak
so vulnerable
Be still
Let God
soothe
calm
restore
as no other force can.

Read Psalm 91

"You will not fear the terror of the night, nor the arrow that flies by day, nor the pestilence that stalks in the darkness, nor the plague that destroys at midday."

Prayer:

Oh, God, I'm so afraid. My fear consumes me. I don't know how to control it. I ask You to take this fear from me. Fill me with Your courage. I know that I can do all things with You as my rock and my encourager. Take me as I am, Lord, weak as a child. Build me up so I can overcome my fears and move into the peace that You give me. I ask You with a full and humble heart. Encourage me, Father. Amen.

Forgiveness

I am sorry
The words stick in my throat wanting to pour forth
Yet waiting somehow
I hold on to the pain and hurt
Why?
I forgive you.
I can whisper the words
I want to say them
but I am waiting for the "I am sorry"
that may never come
Then I remember
"Forgive others as I forgive you"
I am sorry. I forgive you.
The healing begins.

Read 2 Corinthians 5:17-21

"Therefore, if anyone is in Christ, he is a new creation; the old has gone, the new has come."

Prayer:

God, I have sinned against You alone. I'm sorry with all my heart. I give the sin to You. Wipe my heart clean. I know I can't hold on to this sin, Lord, but if I try, please take it from me right now. I accept Your love and forgiveness, Lord, with a humble heart. Even more, I accept Your strength and power to forgive anyone I need to forgive. In You, I can do all things. Thank You for the freedom from sin. Thank You for loving me. Provide the strength to me so I can forgive in order to be Your ambassador. Your forgiveness flows through me to others. Amen.

Gratitude

How wonderful
are the things you have done for me!
How can I ever praise you enough?
If I have my entire life, to eternity and back,
I could not fill the depths of gratitude that I have
for all that you have given to me!
For loving me when I was so much less than lovable
For providing for me in times of want and wealth
For my gifts and for my faults for through them you teach me.
For Your grace, peace, and joy
For your abiding love.

Read Colossians 3:15-17

"And whatever you do, whether in word or deed, do it all in the name of the Lord Jesus, giving thanks to God the Father through him."

Prayer:

Father God, I thank You. I praise Your name for the many blessing You have given to me. I know that all things come from You. I'm so awed by all that You have given to me. My voice rises in the morning to sing praises to You. I carry Your praise on my lips and in my heart all day long. I don't deserve the bounty of Your blessing, Lord. I thank You with a full and over flowing heart for all that You give me. Your love is endless. Your unconditional love sustains me. I will spread that love to everyone I encounter this day. Amen.

Grief

The pain of loss
Pierces my soul
I am immobilized
Everyday tasks seem impossible to perform
Will I ever be able to smile again?
Will the emptiness ever ease?
When will the hole that is my heart be full again?
How mighty is the hurt.

Read Isaiah 61:1-3

"... to comfort all who mourn and provide for those who grieve in Zion- to bestow on them a crown of beauty, instead of ashes, the oil of gladness, instead of mourning, and a garment of praise, instead of a spirit of despair."

Prayer:

Father God, You know the pain in my soul. I grieve with all that I am. The pain is ever present and ever real to me. I can hardly see the light of Your love. I am utterly down and troubled by the loss I feel. Please, Father, comfort me. Hold me in Your loving, caring arms. Provide a balm for my pain. I know that Your love will sustain me, even as I walk down this difficult path. You are there waiting to give me a spirit of praise. I don't need to have all the answers to why this happened. I need to rest in Your love and know that Your will is perfect. Even when I'm in pain, Your love for me will carry me through. The pain is there, and so are You. Thank you, Lord, for weeping with me. Amen.

Guilt

Shame and sorrow
stifle me like a heavy blanket
that I cannot shake off
weariness invades my soul
The shame and the self doubt
take over
Why?
I shout to myself, did I give in?
Why did I hurt myself
And those I love?
And You, Lord, my God,
Why?

Read Psalm 51:1-17

"Have mercy on me, O God, according to your unfailing love; according to your great compassion blot out my transgressions. Wash away all my iniquity, and cleanse me from sin."

Prayer:

Oh, God, how sorry I am. I have sinned. I try to do what is right, but I am weak. I'm so ashamed of my weakness. I want to hide myself from You and to pull away in my shame and sorrow. Your love for me seems so far away when I know that I disappoint You. Thank you for Your grace, which covers every sin that I commit. Please, I ask with a contrite heart. Let your grace pour over me. Wash away my guilt and my sin. Let Your love replace my weakness. Keep me, Father, from sinning again. Please, forgive me. Help me accept Your forgiveness and grace. Strengthen me for the next trial. Help me to be a better child of Yours. Amen.

Happiness

Joy fills my heart
flows up
from a well of living water.
You alone, O God
can fill me with such holy joy.
You alone, O God
can heal me
restore me
basking in Your presence
in the sunlight of happiness
loving you.

Read Philippians 4:11-13

"I am not saying this because I am in need, for I have learned what it is to be content whatever the circumstance."

Prayer:

Dear God, teach me, as You did Paul, to learn true happiness comes from You. Help me not to look at things of this world or to other people to find my happiness. I know Your love is the key to true and lasting joy. I ask You to show me how to embrace Your love even in the midst of a crisis. All things on this earth will pass away, but Your love and joy are eternal. Thank you, God for my happiness. Amen.

Harmony

A balance of life
all things coordinated
joined in perfection
with the perfect one, Jesus
Guide me
as I seek to find peace
in harmony with you,God,
at the pinnacle.

Read Romans 12:9-16

"Live in harmony with one another."

Prayer:

Heavenly Father, I thank you for Your words of guidance on how to live my life. I strive to hear them completely, to take them into my heart, and to live at peace with my brothers and sisters. Please, help me today to remember Your words when I'm faced with conflict, doubt, or fear. Assure me how to be in harmony with all. You help me to achieve peace that surpasses understanding. Lift me up. Thank you, Father for loving me. Amen.

Healing

Despair
overwhelming and complete
takes over my heart, my soul, my mind.
I yield
not to the fears,
but, to You, Lord
reaching for Your perfect plan for me.
I submit myself to you
asking for complete healing
I praise you!
I thank you for loving me so much
I know you have this present pain under control

.

Read 1 Peter 2:23-25

"He himself bore our sins in his body on the tree so that we might die to sin and live for righteousness; by his wounds you have been healed."

Prayer:

God, You are the great physician. The healer of all wounds to the flesh, to the spirit, and to the soul. I'm in need of healing, Lord. I come to You, weak with pain. I ask You to provide me with rest. I know Your will is perfect. My healing will come about as You see what is best for me. Giver of all, give to me what I need to sustain me as I wait. I thank you with all my being for sending Jesus to save me. I will live with You forever healed of all afflictions in the full glory of heaven. Amen.

Hope

I can hold on
to a light
as small as a single lamp
to guide me
because
my hope is in the Lord
who will send what I need
when I need it
at all times
I just have to ask.
The glow of Your light
is all I need.

Read Psalm 42: 5-6

"Why are you so downcast, O my soul? Why so disturbed within me? Put your hope in God for I will yet praise him, my Savior and my God."

Prayer:

Holy Comforter, I'm feeling so hopeless. I come to You with a heavy heart. I don't see a way out. I know that You have a perfect plan for me. I do not need to know every detail. I can rest on Your assurance. You will be there for me, guide me, and lead me home to You at the end of the journey. Give me the hope of a future with You, Lord. Let me know that the present situation is but a step along that path. Amen.

Humility

You give to me all that I am
All that I have
I am nothing without You
Gifts
Talents
Strengths
are not my own but Yours, O God.
I proclaim You as my Lord
and the giver of all
I thank You
from the depths of my being.

Read Micah 6:8

"He has showed you, O man, what is good. And what does the Lord require of you? To act justly, and to love mercy, and to walk humbly with your God."

Prayer:

Dear Father, show me how to do what You require of me with an attitude of humility. All that I have and all that I am comes from You. Help me to keep my pride in check. Help me to give praise and honor to You for what I accomplish. I can often take the credit when I should give homage to You who has given so much to me. I thank you with a heart that is so blessed. I ask You to keep me humble. Know how very grateful I am for Your gifts and Your love. Amen.

Intervention

Enter in, Holy Spirit
Hear my plea
Guide me
Heal me
Move in a small whisper
Rush in a mighty way
Take over for me
Where I cannot
Oh, Spirit, be my Comforter.

Read Romans 8:26-27

"And he who searches our hearts knows the mind of the Spirit, because the Spirit intercedes for the saints in accordance with God's will."

Prayer:

Lord, I come to You with a heart filled with concern and with hope. I don't know how to solve this problem, but You do, Lord. I can rest assured that even when I am weak and feel helpless,You are strong. You offer to carry the problem for me. I ask You to step in, Lord. Take over this burden for me. If I try to take it back, remind me that You are in charge, not me. I know that I can't solve this alone, Lord. You will intervene. Your perfect solution will result. I praise Your name. I thank You with a humble heart. Amen.

Jealousy

The feeling creeps in
at first
unacknowledged
just a slip of a thought
it grows
takes a life of its own
as envy overwhelms,
stifles and stops me
Take this from me!
I cannot bear
to feel this way.

Read Galatians 5:25-26

"Since we live by the Spirit, let us keep in step with the Spirit. Let us not become conceited, provoking and envying each other."

Prayer:

Holy Spirit, come to me. I feel so ashamed of my thoughts and feelings of wanting what another has. Why must I wait? Why must I do without when others seem to have so much? Speak to my jealous heart, Spirit, and cleanse these thoughts from me. I freely give them to You. I ask You to assure me I am loved. I know You have taken care of my needs. I can rest assured You are with me, guiding me to what is right for me. Your love for me is all I need. Amen.

Joy

The radiance shines
from my soul
illuminating my face
lighting up the room
The love of God bubbles forth
overflowing
from the depths of who I am.
Joy is complete
no matter the circumstance,
the sorrow or pain,
Unconditional happiness
wrapped in the love of God.

Read Psalm 126

"The Lord has done great things for us, and we are filled with joy."

Prayer:

God, You have filled the world with such beauty. I stand in awe of Your creation and majesty. I am filled to overflowing from the wealth of joy You provide for me. Make me more aware of all I pass on a daily basis. Show me the depth of joy even when sorrow looms. Allow Your joy to well up inside me and overflow to everyone I meet. There is no substitute for the joy of Your unconditional love and abounding grace. Your joy is my strength. Amen.

Knowledge

I am stopped
waiting for a sign
something tangible
I listen
I yield to You, O God.
Fill my heart with Your wisdom
Show me Your way
that I may stay
in your will.
Help me to be fully armed
with all the knowledge I need
to move as You direct.

Read Proverbs 10:14

"Wise men store up knowledge, but the mouth of a fool invites ruin."

Prayer:

Lord, the knowledge I need for living my life fully and completely is found in Your word and Your teachings. Guide me, Oh Lord, to the truths that are right for me. In every situation, give me the wisdom I need. I seek the way You would have me to go, not my own stubborn course of action. Stop me, Lord, if I choose the wrong path. Lift me up and show me wisdom begins and ends with You. Amen

Longing

The peace of my soul
is disturbed.
I long for a sign,
a message
to fulfill my soul.
I want what I cannot have
I search for what will give me peace,
knowing that You, God, are my hope
my solution.

Read Psalm 119: 81-87

"My soul faints with longing for your salvation, but I have put my hope in your word."

Prayer:

Holy Spirit, I long for something to make my life easier, to give me comfort, and a better way for me to live. I don't see this desire fulfilled. I am frustrated. I have prayed and prayed and still see no answers. Please, Spirit, fill my need. End my longing. Ease my soul. I need help to put my hope in You. In my weakest hours, I find myself resentful and full of self-pity. Take this longing from me. Turn it to hope in You and in Your word. I long for You. Your perfect love is all I need. Amen.

Loneliness

Alone
I stand heavyhearted
burdened with a load to bear
that seems too heavy for one person
Alone
the weight of my cares crush me
I fall
I wait
for You have promised me
that You will carry me through
each day of my life
I never have to be alone again.

Read Luke 5:16
"But Jesus often withdrew to lonely places and prayed."
Prayer:

Father God, the loneliness is overtaking me. I feel so lost and so alone. Even in prayer, I'm having a hard time feeling Your presence. As I pray to You, I ask You to reach into my lonely places. Fill them with Your grace and love. Help me to know that even when I'm alone, You are there. Even when I'm by myself, I'm never alone. Fill me with Your presence. Take this feeling of desolation away from me. As Jesus prayed gratitude to You in the midst of his lonely places, I come to You thankful. Your love will fill my heart where it is empty. Dull the lonely feeling. Replace it with Perfect love. Amen.

Love

To give without expectation
To nurture
Guide
Steer
Admonish
Forgive
Over and over
To rely on the One and only God
Who loves every creature
Unconditionally
In perfect love.

Read 1 Corinthians 13

"Love is patient, love is kind. It does not envy, it does not boast, it is not proud. It is not rude, it is not self-seeking, it is not easily angered, and it keeps no record of wrongs. Love does not delight in evil, but rejoices in the truth. It always protects, always trusts, always hopes, always perseveres."

Prayer:

Loving Father, teach me how to love as You direct. Even more, teach me how to accept the love You wish to pour out on me. I know I'm a sinner. I can do nothing to earn Your love. I don't deserve it. You freely give love to me unconditionally and overflowing. Direct me, Father, how to love others in the same way, so I may fully love as You love me. Amen.

Overwhelmed

Heavy hearted
I struggle
Completion of only the minor duties
Overwhelms
I cannot lift myself
Above the pain
The confusion
Takes over
I am comforted to know
That You feel my pain too
And will provide a solution.

Deuteronomy 31:6

"Be strong and courageous. Do not be afraid or terrified because of them, for the Lord, your God, goes with you: he will never leave you or forsake you."

Prayer:

God of all creation, You are with me through my entire life, the good and the bad. I feel like I can't handle the stress that has been placed upon me. I'm ready to give up. I can't go on. Please, Father, come to me. Help me. I ask You for a solution to this problem. Take the task before me. Guide me to break it down into small manageable parts, so I can see how to solve this as You would have me to solve it. I want to honor You. I thank you for Your help as my burden eases. I can move just one step closer to a solution. Amen.

Patience

Affirmation
Confirmation
Direction
Waiting
Totally giving up control over to God
who is all
knows all
reveals all
in His perfect time.

Read Ecclesiastes 7:8

"The end of a matter is better than it's beginning, and patience is better than pride."

Prayer:

Father God, my patience is running out! I'm feeling like I cannot go on. Please, give me a drink of the everlasting water to restore me and renew me, so I can be more patient in all situations. Let me come to Your well and draw from it when I feel my patience slipping. I can be assured You will give me what I need if I only ask. I'm asking now with a full heart for the renewing spirit of patience. Amen.

Perseverance

To go the distance
To keep on trying
even when the odds
against me seem larger than life
Taking the tasks ahead and
Bit by bit
Finishing one small part of the whole
Letting the Lord strengthen me
Providing the tools needed
to complete me.

Read Hebrews 12:1-3

"Consider him who endured such opposition from sinful men, so that you will not grow weary and lose heart."

Prayer:

Wonderful Savior, You have given me the best gift, the grace and love of God for my sins. Sometimes I feel like giving up, Lord. I know that You felt this way too when You faced the cross. My cross pales in comparison to what You suffered so I could have eternal life. Help me to change my attitude of despair into one of hope. I keep trying to become the person You want me to be and to complete the tasks You set before me. I can do this with You to walk beside me guiding me along the way. Amen.

Praise

The glory of God
Proclaimed
In the iridescent leaf,
Delicate feather,
Breath taking flower,
Every unique face
How majestic!
How awe filled I stand
One small person
a part of life, earth, sky, and seas
Praises rise to the heavens
Alleluia, Amen!

Read Exodus 15:1-2

He is my God and I will praise him, my father's God, and I will exalt him."

Prayer:

Heavenly Father, You are the most high. Your glory and splendor are beyond my imagination. I magnify You and praise Your holy name. I lift my voice in the morning and sing Your praises all the day. As I rest at night, I give thanks to You for all You have provided for me. You are my King. I worship Your majesty. I glorify Your name. Your praise is in my heart and ever on my lips. With humble gratitude, I exalt You. Amen.

Renewal

Cycles of life
Over and over
Provide the faith
to remain steady and strong
Restore my soul
Regain my focus
Renew my hope
in the Lord, my Savior.

Read Isaiah 57:10

"You were wearied by all your ways, but you would not say, 'It is hopeless.' You found renewal of your strength and so you did not faint."

Prayer:

O, God, there are so many times when I can't find the strength to go on. I feel so very helpless and weak in the face of my problems. Take this from me, God. Help me to lean on Your arm as I walk through this valley. All I have to do is take the next step. I know You are holding me up when I can't hold up myself. Thank You for loving me, so I can renew my strength and walk with You once again. Amen.

Resentment

Why? climbs into my thoughts
takes over my reasoning
I don't deserve
to be treated this way
Why?
The anger settles in the pit of my soul
simmering
threatening to boil over into rage
I cry out
with all that I am.
Ease the pain,
Please, help me, Lord.

Read 2 Timothy:22-26

"And the Lord's servant must not quarrel; instead, he must be kind to everyone, able to teach, not resentful."

Prayer:

Dear Holy Spirit, come to me. Ease these feelings of bitterness and jealousy. I know I have a right to be resentful over these circumstances, but if I hold onto to the resentment, it consumes me. I hurt even more. Take Your blanket of comfort. Wrap me in Your arms. Let the feeling I want to hold on to dissipate and flow from me. You are my Comforter and my Restorer. Thank you. Amen.

Rest

Softly falling rain
A gentle wind
Cheerful calls of children
Bright sunshine to warm winter faces
A small drink of God's goodness
Restores
Renews
Refills
Provides the rest we need.

Read Matthew 11:28-30

"Come to me all you who are weary and burdened, and I will give you rest. Take my yoke upon you and learn from me, for I am gentle and humble in heart and you will find rest for your souls. For my yoke is easy, and my burden is light."

Prayer:

Dear Jesus, I am worn out. My body feels drained. I cannot move another step. I come to You with a weary soul in need of restoration and peace. Come to me, dear Lord. Renew my mind, my heart, my body and my soul. I take Your comfort as a warm loving blanket, and wrap myself up in its peace. I know You are the provider of all. You carry my burdens with You. As I release them, the rest I need comes too. Thank you, Loving Lord, thank you. Amen.

Salvation

Your love for me
Is beyond comprehension
Forgive my limited capacity
to understand the depth of love
that would lay down
the life of a son
so I can be forgiven.
Loved to the core of my soul
no matter how weak and sinful I am
The power of the cross
saves and forgives
A gift freely given
I fall to my knees praising my God.

Read 1 Peter 2: 22-25

"He himself bore our sins in his body, on the tree, so that we might die to sins and live for righteousness; by his wounds you have been healed."

Prayer:

Precious Jesus, You suffered and died for my sins. I can't comprehend such a sacrifice of love. It's more than I can understand. I ask You to come into my heart. I accept you as my Lord and my Savior. Let Your love heal my wounds. Show me how to accept Your love unconditionally, so I may pass that same love on to others. I rest assured that You hold a place in heaven for me. I thank You for Your gift of everlasting love. Amen.

Strength

Weakness saps my reserve
to the point of empty
I cannot go on.
Weariness overtakes my bones
small tasks take so much effort.
I sit and wait
letting the love of God creep in,
Filling the hollow spaces with renewed vision
bit by bit
He lifts me up
I can do all things
by His mighty strength!

Read Isaiah 40: 29-31

"He gives strength to the weary and increases the power of the weak. Even young men stumble and fall; but those who hope in the Lord will renew their strength. They will run and not grow weary, they will walk and not be faint."

Prayer:

Heavenly Father, I am weak. I need to wait on You, Lord, as Your word directs. Please, give me the strength to allow You to lead me through this. I'm not strong enough to handle this problem alone, Lord. I rely on You to guide me. Prepare me for the task that lies ahead. Renew my strength, Father. In my weariness, keep my from stumbling. I thank you. Amen.

Temptation

A small voice, a whispered suggestion
A random thought enters
Unaware
And repeats
Urges
Cajoles
Shouts
In my weakness
I do not want to give in
Help me
Strengthen me
My Lord and My Savior.

Read Matthew 26:41

"Watch and pray so that you do not fall into temptation. The spirit is willing but the body is weak."

Prayer:

Dear Lord, help me to resist the temptation before me. I am willing to try, Lord. I am so weak in the face of this obstacle. I ask that You give me the insight to avoid the situations that may cause me to be tempted. In my weakness, I do not want to sin. If I can't avoid the situation, help me, Lord, to be strong in You, to lean on You. Lead me out of the danger I face. I know that You have empathy for me. As You, my Lord, feel the temptations I feel, and You resist them. Teach me to resist. Give me the power to stop when I'm tempted. I fall on my knees calling on your name. Amen.

Thanksgiving

Humble adoration for all that You are
all that You provide for me
I am nothing without my gifts
Everything that You, my heavenly Father, provide for me
From morning to rest time,
You give me all I need if I but ask
With a heart that overflows
I thank you, Lord, for making me
as I am
for loving me in my imperfection
for providing all that I need to praise and honor You.

Read Psalm 100

"Enter his gates with thanksgiving and his courts with praise; give thanks to him and praise his name."

Prayer:

All glory and majesty are given to You, God, the most high. I sing Your praises with a joyful heart. I praise you for the many blessing you provide. You are so awesome and so wonderful! My heart is filled with the glory of You! I kneel before You with reverence. May Your grace to flow over me. Fill me with Your abiding love that endures forever. Amen.

Worry

Nagging doubt
Eats away at my soul
Corrodes my faith
tears away hope
Why can't I remember how precious I am in Your eyes?
You have everything in Your control
I release the worry
Let go and Let You
Take care of me.

Read Matthew 6:25

"Who, by worrying, can add a single hour to hour to his life?"

Prayer:

Holy Spirit, come to me, now. Take this worry away from me. I try to give to You. I take it back again. I know You have my fears and my anxiety under Your control. I need not fear the unknown. You are the Wise Counselor. You know my way even before I ask. Let Your peace and calm assurance flow over me. Let the worry I feel ease and disappear. I surrender all concerns to You, most gracious God. Amen.

Worship

Arms uplifted
Voices united
Instruments resound
Praise to the Lord
Praise to the King
Praise to the Most High Deliverer
Praise To You
The Prince of Peace
The Holy One
In humble adoration
Your children praise You
Our Holy Father.

Read Psalm 95:1-7

"Come, let us bow down in worship, let us kneel before the Lord, our Maker; he is our God and we are the people of his pasture, the flock under his care."

Prayer:

God of all, You are the most high, the Holy One, whom I adore. I come to You filled this day with reverence for all Your creation. You have formed the beings, all the creatures, the beauty and splendor of the land before us. How great is Your majesty! I worship You, God, with all that I am. I'm humbled and awe struck by the creation, power and glory You have formed. Even more, I am so grateful for the grace, forgiveness, and love You pour out on me. I love you, God, with all that I am. Amen.

Guide for Personal Reflection or Small Group Study

You may want to explore these questions to increase your understanding and grow your faith. The answers will be unique to you and help you better understand yourself and our amazing God. There is not one right or wrong answer. You will receive the answer you need according to God's perfect plan. Read the entire chapter of the scripture to grasp the context better. Explore on your own or participate in a small group study with the idea that when two or more gather, God is with them.

I suggest you open your sessions with a prayer to the Holy Spirit for wisdom and discernment. The following pages have room to jot down notes, but you will need more room for a true reflection time.

I have written a leader's guide and a reflection journal. I also offer an email course of video support for each session. You don't need these, as any journal will work for reflecting. Contact me for details: cindybcurtis@iwriteyouwrite.com.

This book has been helpful to those who are going through difficult times. I am humbled and grateful to have repurposed and kept the integrity of the original publication from 2007. The words still hold so much truth.

May your faith increase. May you draw closer to God, your strength, hope, and healer.

Sessions One and Two: Pathways

From the following topics, reflect on these questions:

Acceptance
Change
Direction
Discernment
Harmony

Did you find an answer to a question of direction?

What specifically did you learn from God's word as an answer to a prayer for direction?

What is the difference between acceptance and change?

How can you tell if an answer is yours or God's?

What is the benefit of achieving harmony in your life?

Session Three: Attitudes

From the following topics, reflect on these questions:

Adoration
Encouragement
Gratitude
Happiness
Praise

When have you felt the most humbled by the majesty of God?

How do you find the encouragement you need to live your life as a bold Christian?

How do you express gratitude in the midst of pain?

How is it possible to experience happiness at all times?

When do you feel like praising God the most?

Session Four: Emotions

From the following topics, reflect on these questions:

Anger
Fear
Grief
Jealousy
Resentment

When has anger caused you to act irrationally?

When have you been more afraid of the thought of something rather than the actual event?

Why is grief so difficult?

What are some positives about the process of grief?

When can jealousy and resentment teach you a better way?

Session Five: Grateful

From the following topics, reflect on these questions:

Blessing
Faith
Hope
Love
Thanksgiving

What do you consider to be a blessing from God?

What is the best way for you to grow your faith?

How do you hold on to hope when tragedy strikes?

Why is it difficult to accept God's love? To give God's love?

How can you embrace the mighty love God has for you?

What is the difference between thanksgiving and giving?

Session Six: Choices

From the following topics, reflect on these questions:

Comfort
Knowledge
Patience
Perseverance
Strength

How have you felt the comfort of God through others?

How can you gain knowledge?

When do you need to pray for patience?

How can you keep on trying when times are difficult?

How can you feel strong when you are feeling so very weak?

Session Seven: Focus

From the following topics, reflect on these questions:

Conflict
Confusion
Doubt
Guilt
Overwhelmed

How are you to handle conflict within the church or with other Christians?

What do you when you are confused?

How do you overcome doubt?

What causes you to feel guilty?

How does God direct you to deal with guilt?

What is the best way to proceed when you are overwhelmed?

Session Eight: Self-care

From the following topics, reflect on these questions:

Discipline
Intervention
Longing
Renewal
Rest

When is it hard to accept God's discipline?

How do you intervene on behalf of a family member or someone who does not know the Lord?

How can you satisfy your longings to be in line with what God wants and allows for you?

Why are rest and renewal so important?

How can you make self-care a priority?

Session Nine: Trust

From the following topics, reflect on these questions:

Forgiveness
Healing
Loneliness
Temptation
Worry

Why is it so difficult to forgive those who aren't sorry for their behavior?

How can holding on to unforgiveness prevent your healing?

What are some solutions for dealing with loneliness?

How does worry affect you?

How can you keep for worrying?

Session Ten: Completion

From the following topics, reflect on these questions:

Confession
Humility
Joy
Salvation
Worship

What does confession do for you?

What are you hiding that needs to be put before God?

How can you remain humble when you are praised, recognized, and affirmed?

What is the difference between happiness and joy?

Have you prayed the prayer of salvation? Why? Why not?

What changes will you put into place to worship God with all of your being?

Don't miss out!

Visit the website below and you can sign up to receive emails whenever Cindy Barrineau Curtis publishes a new book. There's no charge and no obligation.

https://books2read.com/r/B-A-WADY-RISYE

BOOKS 2 READ

Connecting independent readers to independent writers.

About the Author

Cindy Barrineau Curtis is a Master teacher, published author, and motivational speaker. Her career spans over 30 years in education, ministry, writing, and speaking. Her writing offers hope and empowers readers with methods to manage life's ups and downs with confidence and grace as they grow in faith. Her fiction entertains and inspires.

She combines her experience designing curriculum and instruction with her own writing goals, creative writing, poetry, and photography.

She offers writing tips and workshops for all ages.

Contact her at cbc@cindybcurtis.com

Read more at https://cindybcurtis.com.

www.ingramcontent.com/pod-product-compliance
Lightning Source LLC
LaVergne TN
LVHW090536110826
845146LV00003B/1134

9798988450924